Monetizing Podcasts
How to Use Social Media Marketing

Table of Contents

The future of communicating with customers rests in engaging with them through every possible channel: phone, e-mail, chat, Web, and social networks. Customers are discussing a company's products and brand in real time. Companies need to join the conversation.

— Marc Benioff

Chapter 1. Introduction

Step into the world of podcasting with our Special Report: "Monetizing Podcasts: How to Use Social Media Marketing". This delightful, comprehensive guide is your roadmap to generating a considerable income through one of the most rapidly growing media channels - Podcasts. The magic lies in harnessing the power of social media as a marketing tool, transforming your podcast into a revenue-generating venture easily and effectively. Whether you're a media veteran or an enthusiastic beginner eager to turn your podcasting passion into profit, this Special Report is your golden ticket. Ignite your entrepreneurial spirit, let it flitter across this riveting read, and seize the opportunity to master the art and business of podcasting. Get ready to fuel your podcasting journey with success and cheers by grabbing this Special Report today!

Chapter 2. Understanding the Podcast Landscape

In the ever-evolving world of digital technology, podcasting has emerged as a potent medium that has blurred geographical boundaries and expanded the reach of audio content like never before. Despite the increasing complexity of our digital landscape, this booming platform has witnessed a surge in popularity and scope, owing to its unique flexibility and personalized user experience.

2.1. The Definition of Podcasting

Podcast is a digital audio file which can be streamed or downloaded from the internet. Unlike traditional radio, a podcast doesn't adhere to a specific time schedule and is not confined to a particular geographic local. Rather, it can be listened to anywhere, anytime, often on portable devices like smartphones or computers. Podcasts usually come as a series where new installments are automatically received by subscribers. The term is an amalgam of "iPod" - a popular portable media player by Apple, and "broadcast". The arrival of Apple's iTunes Store in 2005 fostered the spread of podcasting, making it a widely accepted form of delivering audio content to a global audience.

2.2. Evolution of Podcasting and Its Reach

From being virtually unheard of in the early 2000s to becoming a ubiquitous part of today's digital culture, the growth of podcasting is nothing short of phenomenal. Since its humble beginnings, podcasting has grown steadily and consistently over the past decade. The convenience of on-demand listening, proliferation of smartphones, and the growth in time spent commuting contributed to its rising popularity.

The rise of podcasting isn't limited to a specific region or demography. It has overleaped geographical boundaries, appealing to a vast audience spanning continents. According to studies, podcasts reach over 100 million Americans every month, with global numbers being significantly larger. This shows that podcasts, with their unique blend of storytelling and information sharing mechanism, are a worldwide phenomenon, with a significant percentage of the global population tuning in.

2.3. Podcast Genres and Categories

Podcast content is as diverse as the audience it connects with. There are podcasts covering almost any topic imaginable - from politics to philosophy, business to education, health and wellness to comedy and entertainment, and much more. This wide variety of content caters to listeners of all ages, interests, and backgrounds, ultimately fuelling the popularity of podcasting.

2.4. Understanding Podcast Listeners

The listeners are what truly shape the podcast landscape. In general, podcast listeners are avid learners, receptive to new ideas, and appreciate deep, nuanced discussions. They value the freedom that podcasts provide to consume content at their own pace, in their own time and the ability to delve into topics they are passionate about, irrespective of how niche those might be. You'll find them multi-tasking, as they listen to their favorite podcasts while commuting, exercising, cooking, or before falling asleep.

2.5. The Business Perspective: Podcasting as a Marketing Tool

From a business perspective, podcasting represents an excellent marketing opportunity. Apart from the ability to reach a wide and engaged audience, podcasts allow businesses to connect with their audience on a personal level. Owing to the intimate nature of audio, podcast listeners often build a deep connection and trust with the podcast host. Businesses can leverage this trust to foster a more personal relationship with their customers, steadily turning listeners into loyal brand advocates.

Chapter 3. The Rise of Podcasts: A Historical Overview

The podcast landscape, as we experience it today, did not appear in the blink of an eye. It is the product of decades of technological advancements, growing content platforms, and shifting listener preferences. As we trace the historical development of podcasts, we unfold a compelling narrative of progress, adaptation, and persistence that shines a spotlight on how this relatively nascent medium has cemented its place in the global communication industry.

3.1. The Dawn of Podcasting

The inception of podcasts harks back to the 1980s — a time interspersed with rapid technological developments. It was during this decade that the concept of downloadable radio-style shows first emerged, although they were initially confined to tech-savvy communities. The first semblance of a podcast was an audio blog. Programmers and technology enthusiasts would record themselves discussing various topics, encode these recordings into digital files, and share them via download links or emails. However, without simple, unified platforms for distribution or a widespread internet audience, these audio blogs remained niche.

3.2. The term 'Podcast': A Twist of Fate

In the early 2000s, the sensation of MP3 players, led by Apple's iPod, was rapidly gaining traction. Simultaneously, the world was transitioning toward a digital revolution, and a neologism was bound to occur. The term 'podcast' - a portmanteau of 'iPod' and 'broadcast'- was coined in 2004 by journalist Ben Hammersley. Despite this, many people think that 'podcast' means 'Portable On Demand broadcast', which reflects the content's ability to be consumed as and when the listener wishes.

3.3. RSS and its Contribution

One fundamental development in the early 2000s was the refinement of RSS (Really Simple Syndication) technology. Created by Dave Winer and improved by a team including Adam Curry, this technology allowed audio files to be attached to RSS feeds (a feature called enclosures), setting the stage for what would become routine podcast distribution. When subscribed to a feed, users would receive new files automatically, facilitating an easy and convenient way of delivering audio content — podcasting in embryonic form.

3.4. The Impact of iTunes

Apple's release of iTunes 4.9 in 2005, which featured integrated podcasting capabilities, was a pivotal moment in podcast history. Podcasts could now reach a vast audience, breaking free from their niche status. This milestone not only helped confirm the term 'podcast', but also democratized the creation and consumption of podcast content. The iTunes platform acted as a springboard, launching podcasting into a period of exponential growth, which continues unabated to this day.

3.5. Expansion and Monetization

With the advent of smartphones and the proliferation of mobile internet, podcasting began to see steady growth from 2008 onward. Ever-more sophisticated recording equipment, editing software, and distribution platforms led to increased production quality, while the continued growth of the internet audience propelled listenership. Consumer brands and businesses started seeing the potential for marketing and monetizing podcasts, leading to an array of strategies such as sponsorships, branded content, and subscription models.

The integration of podcasting services into music streaming platforms like Spotify and Amazon Music, and the development of dedicated platforms such as PodcastOne, Stitcher, and Luminary, further bolstered the podcasting landscape. In recent years, we have seen big media companies, content producers, celebrities, and individuals alike adopt podcasting, affirming its dominance as an essential component in our media diet.

3.6. Present Day and Future Directions

Today, podcasting is a booming industry flaunting a roster of a broad array of genres. It's estimated that there are over two million active podcasts, with millions of episodes in over 100 languages. Podcasts have become a significant force in mitigating geographical, cultural, and language barriers and have unlocked novel opportunities for advertising, storytelling, and learning. As the next frontier of podcasting unfolds, we will undoubtedly see the continued integration of technology, such as artificial intelligence and virtual reality, propelling an even more immersive podcasting experience.

Venturing through the historical overview of podcasts' rise, we've witnessed a fascinating amalgamation of technological advancements and societal shifts coming together to give life to this explosive medium. Without a doubt, the podcast, in all its diversity and ubiquity, stands as a testament to human communication's evolving nature. In the realm of digital content, it epitomizes a cause célèbre. It interweaves the simplicity of the spoken word with the complexity of global distribution, creating a medium that unites millions, empowering conversations and narratives that echo worldwide. This historical sketch illustrates how far we've come and fuels our curiosity for what lays ahead in the dynamic world of podcasting.

Chapter 4. Crafting Your Unique Podcast Content

In an era of ever-evolving online content, crafting a unique podcast to stand out from the crowd is a significant task and requires a thorough understanding of various elements. This chapter aims to shed light on these aspects.

4.1. Understanding Your Objectives

Identifying your goals at the very start is paramount. Whether your podcast aspires to entertain, to inform, or to inspire, having a clear objective not only directs your content development but also helps in attracting the right audience. Is your podcast intended to be educational, covering academic content? Or would you rather it be light-hearted and humorous? The answers to these questions effectively set the foundation for your podcast content.

4.2. Identifying Your Audience

No content can succeed without resonating with its intended audience. With podcasts, the audience is your heartbeat. Take time to understand who your audience is and what they desire. Analyzing demographics, interests, listening habits and more is a crucial step toward crafting content that matches their tastes. Always remember that you are crafting your podcast not just for yourself, but for your audience.

4.3. Settling on a Podcast Format

Formulating a unique podcast format requires a careful dissection of different format options and understanding which one would go well with your objectives and audience. The format might be an interview style, solo commentary, panel discussion, or narrative storytelling. Your choice should depend on what feels natural, aligns with the podcast's intent, and resonates with your audience.

4.4. Sculpting a Unique Style and Voice

Crafting a unique podcast also involves establishing a distinctive style and voice. Think about what tone and language suit your content and audience. The audio design - the music, sound effects, and sonic branding - also play a vital role in setting the mood and creating an immersive listening experience. The style and voice should create an audio identity that is reminiscent of your brand's essence.

4.5. Consistency is Key

Regular and consistent publication of podcast episodes fosters a loyal and engaged audience. Once you've established a publishing schedule that aligns with your content creation capabilities, stick to it. If your listeners know they can rely on a new episode every week, fortnight, or month, they are more likely to stay engaged and loyal.

4.6. Quality Over Quantity

While consistency is essential, so too is quality. Podcasting is a medium where content is paramount. Focus on delivering content-driven by quality, be it audio or the narration. Investing in good audio equipment and thorough content research and planning can significantly improve the quality of your podcast.

4.7. Capitalize on Guest Appearances

Guest appearances can add value to your podcast by bringing in expert perspectives and broadening your reach. However, ensure that your guest aligns with your podcast's theme and can contribute to a meaningful conversation.

4.8. Evaluating and Evolving Your Content

Podcasting is not one-size-fits-all. It's essential to regularly evaluate, iterate, and evolve your content based on listener feedback and performance analytics. Respond to reviews, track listener statistics, and be ready to mix things up if something isn't resonating.

Unique podcast content is not merely about being different but about being valuable and impactful. In the following chapters, we delve into harnessing this uniqueness through social media marketing and turning your podcast into a financially lucrative venture - stay tuned!

Chapter 5. Demystifying Social Media Marketing

Social media marketing can feel like an unfathomable concept shrouded in mystery, a bewildering labyrinth of trending hashtags, algorithms, and followers. However, as seemingly perplexing it may seem, understanding its fundamental framework and meticulously harnessing its power can act as a springboard, enabling your podcast to permeate the spectrum of listeners, thereby setting a strong foundation for monetization.

5.1. Unraveling the Concept of Social Media Marketing

Primarily, the essence of social media marketing revolves around crafting a strategic blueprint to lure an audience using various social media platforms. As such, it involves curating engaging content, monitoring user reactions and engagement, analyzing the outcomes, and embedding advertisements and sponsored content where necessary. The core purpose here is to spawn a close-knit community of interactive listeners and ardent followers who eagerly await your podcast's releases.

5.2. Pearls of Strategic Communication

In stark contrast to traditional advertising, social media marketing is centered more on interactive communication, facilitating dialogues between the host and the audience. This engagement act as the lifeblood of your podcast, fueling increased listens and shares, thereby driving your podcast rankings upwards. By interacting with your audience, not only do you foster a sense of familiarity and loyalty, but you also receive real-time feedback to help hone your podcast's future episodes.

5.3. The Intricate Web of Algorithms

Social media platforms utilize extraordinary complex algorithms that exhibit preferences to content that resonates well with their users. Understanding these algorithms can be instrumental in escalating your podcast's exposure,numerous listens, and potential monetization. Each social media bullhorn - Facebook, Instagram, Twitter, or LinkedIn - has its unique algorithms, involving distinct components like engagement, relevance, and recency. Capturing such a nuanced comprehension necessitates persistent learning and observation.

5.4. Craft of Content Curation

Content is indeed the king in the realm of social media marketing. An amplifier of your podcast's voice, your social media content can significantly influence the potency of your podcast's reach. Incorporating a mix of promotions, insights, behind-the-scenes, and engagement posts can ensure that your audience finds value in following your social media accounts. Conjuring diversely interesting content while ensuring a balanced post frequency is crucial in maintaining an engaged follower base.

5.5. Astute Adapting to Changing Trends

The arena of social media is a dynamic one, brimming with rapidly morphing trends. Astute podcasters adapt swiftly to these changes, incorporating them into their social media strategy. Understanding and leveraging these trends can catapult your podcast towards widespread recognition and ensuing monetary gains. By attuning your ears to the social media ground, you can rein in your audience's interests, thereby prompting them to tune in to your podcasts.

5.6. Deciphering Analytics

One of the vital elements of social media marketing lies in the gold mines of data - 'Analytics'. Every engagement on social media leaves a data trail. By probing into the data, you can vividly comprehend your audience's preferences, the time they mostly engage, their demographics, and the performance benchmarks of your posts. Such knowledge can guide your content creation, social media strategies, and monetization techniques to target the right chord of audience psyche effectively.

5.7. Paid Promotions: A Strategic Weapon

The fierce competition within the virtual space makes visibility a challenging pursuit. Paid promotions can act as strategic aces up your sleeve to overcome this hurdle. By sponsoring your podcast posts, you can guarantee views and reach out to potential listeners beyond your organic followers. This strategy, although involving an initial investment, can be profitable in the long run as your listenership spirals, leading to more substantial monetization opportunities.

5.8. The Power of Partnerships

Lastly, adopting the power of partnerships by collaborating with influencers, brands, or other similar podcasters can be an effective strategy in elevating your podcast's recognition. These partnerships can be mutually beneficial, granting both parties exposure to a broader audience base. By strategizing collaborations wisely, you can significantly drive your podcast's social media engagement, scope of reach, and monetization.

Understanding and implementing social media marketing strategies might seem like an intimidating task, yet it offers gargantuan potential benefits in terms of listenership and monetization for your podcast. It doesn't demand you to be a marketing maven but rather an enthusiast, eager to learn, adapt, and implement with tenacity and perseverance. One stride at a time, one post at a time, you can successfully steer your podcast's social media journey towards sustainable growth and profitable monetization.

Chapter 6. The Role of Social Media in Podcast Monetization

Let's delve deep into the fascinating realm of podcast monetization through social media. This is a vast subject that intricately interlaces two of the most exciting and rapidly evolving media channels, podcasting and social media, and hints at a synergistic relationship that results in effective monetization strategies.

6.1. The Conceptual Alignment of Podcasts and Social Media

Imagine social media as a perpetually bustling marketplace and your podcast as a unique shop within this marketplace. Every social media user is a potential customer who can stop by your shop, and if they like what they hear, can become your listener, your patron, potentially lending to your monetary success. The key to leveraging this reality is understanding the fundamental alignment of podcasts and social media.

Both podcasting and social media thrive on the sharing of ideas and information. They both have an inherent aspect of community and interactivity. Podcast listeners often want to engage with podcast creators, discuss shared interests, and explore new ideas, something made incredibly easy with the use of social media. This conceptual alignment not only enhances the reach of podcasts but increases their chances of monetization given the right strategies.

6.2. The Dynamics of Social Media in Driving Podcast Revenue

Social media's role in driving podcast revenue is dynamic and manifold. Its chief aspect is increasing listener reach. The success of a podcast, like any other product, largely depends on its audience size. The larger the audience, the higher the chances of monetization.

Different social media platforms reach different demographic groups, but collectively, they cater to a wide range of users spanning various age groups, interests, geographies, and cultural backgrounds. By strategically positioning your podcast on social media, you can achieve widespread reach, eventually leading to increased listeners and potential revenues.

Social media also helps in creating listener loyalty through direct and regular engagement, which impacts the long-term sustainability of podcast monetization. Strategies such as regular posts, engaging content, behind-the-scenes snaps, polls, Q&A sessions, etc., can help with audience retention, driving regular listens and eventually aiding monetization.

Importantly, social media acts as an excellent platform for direct monetization through sponsored posts, collaborations, and ad revenues. You can partner with brands and businesses that align with your podcasts, offering them promotional spaces within your podcast or on your social media posts. This partnership model serves as a direct monetization pathway.

6.3. Intricacies of Monetization Tactics for Different Social Media Platforms

Each social media platform has unique characteristics that can be leveraged for podcast monetization.

Facebook allows for the creation of dedicated pages and groups for your podcast. You can engage with your audience, conduct live sessions, share podcast snippets, and run ad campaigns. It also lets you integrate paid subscription models.

Instagram, with its visually-appealing interface, is a great platform for sharing engaging images, short videos, IGTV episodes, and live content related to your podcast. Instagram stories can keep your listeners informed about new episodes and upcoming engagements. Instagram's shopping feature can also be used to sell podcast merchandise.

LinkedIn is an excellent platform if your podcast centers around career, industry insights, entrepreneurship, or professional skills. LinkedIn's promotion features further aid in reaching a wider professional audience.

Twitter's microblogging nature suits real-time, quick updates about your podcast. Regular tweets, retweets, and hashtag usage can result in organic growth of your podcast's reach.

Knowing which platform aligns with your target audience's consumption behavior is essential for implementing monetization strategies effectively.

6.4. Harnessing the Power of Analytics for Maximizing Monetization

Monetization efforts should be aided by a strong understanding of analytics. Social media platforms offer robust analytics tools that reflect user engagement, post interactions, and audience dynamics. These metrics allow podcasters to understand their audience better and shape their social media marketing efforts, thereby maximizing the potential for monetization.

For instance, your Instagram insights might show that behind-the-scenes content gets more engagement, hinting at the path of content strategy. Facebook's ad performance metrics could help reorient your ad campaign, affecting your podcast's reach and potential direct monetization through promotions.

Indeed, podcast monetization through social media isn't a mere prospect—it's an exciting reality, a formidable combination of strategic moves and analytical insight. It's an art form, where nuances of both podcasting and social media should be harnessed at its best. By treating your podcast as more than just a content offering and incorporating a robust, intuitive social media strategy, you can tap into profitable pathways that redefine your podcasting journey.

Chapter 7. Strategic Planning: Creating Your Social Media Marketing Plan

Strategic planning is critical in any endeavour that involves public engagement, and social media marketing for podcasts is no exception. This chapter delves deep into the methodical process of creating an effective social media marketing plan for your podcast. It takes you on a detailed journey, interpreting the discrete steps involved and giving a bird's eye view on how each step fits into the bigger picture.

7.1. Identifying Your Objectives

The first step in creating your social media marketing plan involves identifying your objectives. This is the 'what' of your entire plan; what you aim to achieve through your podcast and social media engagement. Your objectives could be related to expanding your listenership, increasing subscriber numbers, establishing your podcast as a thought leader in your niche, promoting a product or service, or any combination of these. Make sure your objectives are clear, measurable, achievable, relevant, and time-bound (SMART). This clarity is vital, as having tangible goals can keep you focused and motivated, and also aids in tracking your progress.

7.2. Understanding Your Target Audience

The second step is to understand your target audience - 'who' you are focusing your podcast towards. This involves researching demographics, preferences, tastes, needs, habits, and social media usage patterns. The more you understand your target audience, the better you can tailor your podcast content and your marketing approach to resonate with them and hold their interest.

7.3. Selecting the Right Social Media Platforms

Next, you must select the 'where' - the social media platforms where you will establish your podcast's presence. This choice should be based on where your target audience spends most of their time. Popular platforms include Facebook, Instagram, Twitter, and LinkedIn, each of which comes with their own unique features and considerations. It is key to understand these nuances and how they align with your objectives and audience to make an informed choice.

7.4. Creating Valuable and Engaging Content

Now comes the 'what' - the content. Your social media posts should not just be about promoting your podcast episodes. They should offer value, provoke thought, entertain, educate, or inspire. Share behind-the-scenes glimpses, highlight audience feedback, conduct polls, post teasers and snippets from your episodes, share relevant industry news and updates, and engage with your audience. Remember that content quality is more important than quantity. Pets adherence to your brand's voice, tone, and aesthetics is paramount in maintaining a cohesive brand identity.

7.5. Scheduling and Frequency of Posts

Once you have your content, decide on the 'when'- the frequency of your posts, and the best times to post. Using insights from your social media platform, find out when your audience is most active. Regularity and predictability in your posting schedule can help you maintain a steady presence and keep your audience engaged.

7.6. Tracking, Analyzing, and Tweaking Your Plan

Finally, you need to focus on the 'how well' aspect, that involves tracking and analyzing the effectiveness of your plan using the analytics tools provided by most social media platforms. This step is crucial to understand if you're achieving your goals, and to identify areas that need tweaking or changing. Regular analysis, followed by necessary modifications, ensures your social media marketing plan stays dynamic, relevant, and effective in the long run.

A successful social media marketing plan for podcasters is a veritable treasure map to better engagement, increased listenership, and ultimately, higher monetization. As you hold this map in your hands, bear in mind that the journey will be marked with experiments, learning, changes, and evolution. After all, it's the thrill and knowledge gained from the journey, not just the treasure itself, that makes you a true adventurer.

Chapter 8. Mastering Different Social Platforms: Facebook, Instagram, Twitter and LinkedIn

Recognizing and harnessing the unique attributes of the various social media platforms is crucial to your podcast's success. Appreciating the nuances, individual user behaviors and content preferences for each platform will aid in creating a comprehensive social media strategy that drives audience growth and podcast monetization. This extends to platforms such as Facebook, Instagram, Twitter, and LinkedIn, each possessing distinctive attributes that make them crucial cogs in your marketing machine. Let's delve into detailed explorations of these platforms, providing comprehensive, in-depth instructions on how to effectively utilize them for your podcast promotion and monetization.

8.1. Understanding Facebook for Podcast Promotion

Facebook is a diverse social platform catering to a wide array of age groups, boasting over 2.8 billion active users. This presents a near-infinite pool of potential podcast listeners. Its features such as Groups, Pages, and paid advertising offer multifaceted avenues for promoting your podcast.

1. **Facebook Pages:** The primary vessel for any business venture on Facebook, creating a Page for your podcast is the first step. This serves as your podcast's central hub where listeners can find episodes, behind-the-scenes content, or communicate directly with the host. Be mindful to regularly update your Page to keep

listeners engaged.

2. **Facebook Groups:** Working symbiotically with your Page, a Facebook Group can foster a community around your podcast. It allows listeners to engage in discussions, share opinions, and provides you the opportunity to gather valuable feedback and data.

3. **Facebook Ads:** Advertisements can extend your reach beyond organic growth, targeting specific demographics or locations. Although requiring a budget, Facebook Ads are extremely flexible, allowing customization based on your objectives and budget.

8.2. Navigating Instagram for Podcast Promotion

Instagram, unlike Facebook, is a platform driven by visual content. This necessitates a different approach, aiming to create visually enticing content that entices potential listeners. Utilize a variety of features like Posts, Stories, Reels or IGTV to showcase your podcast.

1. **Posts & IGTV:** Regularly post content related to your podcast. This could range from stunning artwork and branded images to snippets of your episodes in video form on IGTV.

2. **Stories & Reels:** Keep your audience engaged with temporary Stories which could include behind-the-scenes content or sneak peeks into future episodes. Explore the creative potential of Reels, which could repurpose enjoyable moments from your podcast into digestible, entertaining segments.

3. **Instagram Ads:** Similar to Facebook, Instagram Ads hold significant potential in broadening your reach. From Stories to IGTV, Instagram allows you to advertise on multiple fronts.

8.3. Implementing Twitter for Podcast Promotion

Twitter, a platform characterized by its brevity and real-time interaction, offers an exceptional platform for promoting your podcast. Posting consistent, engaging tweets and participating in appropriate hashtags can create a buzz around your podcast.

1. **Live-Tweeting & Hashtags:** Live-tweet during your podcast recording, providing fun insights or teasers, and encourage listener interaction with relevant hashtags. This often helps in creating discussion threads, fostering community engagement.

2. **Twitter Chats:** Participate in Twitter Chats related to your podcast field. This positions you as a thought leader and helps draw attention to your content.

3. **Promoted Tweets:** If you have some budget to spare, Promoted Tweets can help get your podcast in front of a larger audience.

8.4. Harnessing LinkedIn for Podcast Promotion

LinkedIn, primarily a professional networking site, has branched out into content creation and sharing, making it another potential platform for podcast promotion, best suited for podcasts in the business, tech, or professional development niches.

1. **Quality Content & Networking:** Share insightful, valuable content from your podcast that caters to professionals and industry leaders. Engage in networking, linking your podcast to relevant groups or discussions.

2. **LinkedIn Articles & Videos:** Utilize LinkedIn's native articles and video features to share long-form content such as episode summaries, key takeaways or thought leadership pieces.

3. **Sponsored Content:** LinkedIn's sponsored content feature allows you to promote your podcast posts to a wider, pinpointed professional audience.

Each platform harbors its particular strengths and understanding these subtleties is paramount in aligning your social media approach. Beyond understanding, consistency, engagement, and a degree of experimentation will go a long way in helping you master these platforms and subsequently, elevate your podcast to unrealized heights.

Chapter 9. Establishing Your Podcast Brand on Social Media

In an era that breathes the air of digitization effusively, the role of social media in establishing your podcast brand is pivotal and cannot be overstated. Amplifying your online presence isn't simply about creating accounts across all platforms; it's a meticulous process of understanding how each social media channel can be leveraged to reinforce your brand, growing a loyal audience base, and fostering engagement to better humanize your podcast brand.

9.1. Understanding Your Brand Identity

The journey to establish your podcast brand on social media begins with understanding your brand identity—what your brand stands for, your unique style, your values, your voice. It involves meticulously carving out a unique niche based on your podcast's style, theme, and targeted listener demographics. Carefully cultivate your value proposition—define what sets your podcast apart from others, and why listeners should choose your podcast over the countless others available.

Once you've solidified your brand identity, it's crucial to consistently radiate these aspects across your social media platforms. This does not simply mean using the same logo or colors across platforms, although consistency in visual elements is key. More importantly, it refers to maintaining your unique tone, voice, style, and philosophies, manifesting your brand identity through every caption, image, hashtag, interaction, and piece of content you share.

9.2. Building an Engaging Online Presence

To establish your podcast brand on social media, it's crucial to build an engaging online presence. Start with creating compelling content that aligns with your brand identity and resonates with your target audience.

Consistency in posting is another crucial aspect. Develop a content calendar to ensure you're frequently updating your social media profiles with relevant and engaging content. Regular updates not only give your followers something to look forward to but also increase your visibility and improve your engagement rates.

Another effective strategy is to leverage user-generated content, as it can offer social proof and foster a sense of community among followers. Similarly, collaborations with influencers or other podcasters in your niche can broaden your reach and strengthen your brand.

9.3. Harnessing Different Social Media Platforms

Each social media platform has its unique intricacies, audience base, and content types. Identify the platforms your audience frequents the most and make sure you maximize your brand visibility on those.

For example, platforms like Instagram and Pinterest highly value visually appealing content. For these platforms, vibrant behind-the-scenes images, infographics, or podcast clip visuals can create an engaging feed. Platforms like Twitter and LinkedIn, on the other hand, thrive on informational content, debates, and professional networking. Hence, sharing your podcast episodes, blog articles, or news about your podcast can help to engage your audience on these platforms.

9.4. Implementing Effective Social Media Strategies

Effective promotion and marketing strategies are integral to building your podcast brand on social media. Cross-promotion, where you promote your podcast across multiple social media platforms, can be beneficial in expanding your reach. Additionally, teasers of upcoming podcast episodes can create anticipation among your listeners.

Another crucial aspect is to encourage listeners to engage with your content. Ask questions, and prompt discussions in your posts. More engagement often leads to increased visibility due to the algorithm of many social media platforms.

Moreover, don't forget to use the appropriate hashtags (#) along with your posts as they can increase your content visibility and findability for users who don't yet follow your podcast.

9.5. Engaging with Your Audience

Finally, building a brand isn't merely about broadcasting your message. It's about building relationships. Respond to comments, thank your followers for their support, and make efforts to make your brand more approachable and human. In addition, ensure you manage any negative comments or criticisms gracefully and constructively, as this can greatly affect public perception of your brand.

In conclusion, establishing your podcast brand on social media is a strategic process involving understanding your brand identity, creating engaging content, leveraging different platforms, implementing promotional strategies, and staying engaged with your audience. By perennially evolving in sync with social media trends and pulse of your audience while maintaining the unique essence of your brand, you can successfully make a mark in the podcast landscape. As you embark on this journey, remember that every 'like', 'share', 'comment', or 'follow' is a building block towards establishing your podcast brand, each helping to construct a robust and dynamic edifice of your brand's presence that resonates impressively across the digital universe.

Chapter 10. Engaging With Audience: Building and Retaining Listenership

Engaging with your listenership is not just a paramount task but a journey that needs to be carried out with utmost vigor and diligence. A successful podcast is an engaging podcast. It's not only the quality of your content that matters but also the relationship you build with your audience. Your listeners are your most valuable resource, and your engagement with them can significantly influence your podcast's success and its potential for monetization.

10.1. Understanding Your Audience

Understanding your audience largely revolves around knowing who they are, what they are interested in, and how they engage with your podcast. Guest selection, episode themes, duration, all hinge on your listener's preferences. Analytics tools like Google Analytics can help you delve deeper into demographics and audience behavior. You can also survey your audience directly through social media platforms, email, or even directly in your podcast.

10.2. Interactive Content

A proven way to engage your audience is by creating interactive content, which spurs them to take immediate action. Social media allows for dynamic conversation and feedback in real-time. Consider Live sessions on platforms like Facebook or Instagram, where your listeners can participate in discussions. Social media polls, contests, and Q&A sessions further involve listeners and make them feel valued.

10.3. Social Media Engagement

Social media does not just provide a platform to share your podcast but helps nurture audience relationships. Regularly posting valuable content on social media can drive engagement and expand your reach. Use compelling visuals, intriguing captions, hashtags, and share behind-the-scenes content to create intrigue and excitement.

10.4. Managing Negative Feedback

Negative feedback is inevitable but, handled well, can become an avenue for improvement. Assess the feedback, acknowledge the issue, and respond professionally. Apologize if necessary and assure the audience of a solution. Honesty and transparency often attract respect and loyalty.

10.5. Celebrity Engagement

Partnering with influencers or industry experts can boost your podcast's visibility. Their social validation can attract a larger audience and enhance credibility. Include their insights in your podcast and share their endorsements on your social platforms.

10.6. Listener Accessibility

Easy access to your podcast is critical in continuing audience engagement. Ensure your podcast is available across various platforms, and provide easy-to-follow instructions on your social media for new listeners on how to access episodes.

10.7. Audience Involvement

Seek ways to involve the audience in your podcast. You could accept content suggestions, answer listener's queries during episodes, or even include listeners' stories in your podcast. This form of involvement minimizes the distance between you and your audience, leading to stronger bonds.

10.8. Direct Communication

Providing avenues for direct communication goes a long way in maintaining loyal listenership. Answer direct messages, comments, and consistently acknowledge your audience's input. Email newsletters also offer a personalized way to stay connected with your listeners, update them with your latest episodes, guests, and other relevant content.

10.9. Podcast Community

Cultivate a podcast community for your listeners. Social media groups, forums, or meet-ups provide spaces for listeners to mingle and share their thoughts about your podcast. It acts as an engagement hub that perpetuates discussion about your podcast even in your absence.

10.10. Consistent Branding

Maintain consistency in your branding on all platforms, from logos and colors to language and tone. Consistent branding goes a long way in building brand recognition, which in turn can lead to higher listener engagement and loyalty.

Implementing these strategies for audience engagement can effectively convert listeners into loyal fans and brand ambassadors. Building and maintaining strong relationships with your audience is not a one-time effort but constant work that pays off in brand loyalty, word-of-mouth marketing, and subsequently, monetization.

Chapter 11. Practical Tips: From Monetization Strategies to Implementation

Creating a revenue stream from your podcast involves much more than merely recording and uploading content. To succeed in attracting advertisers or sponsors and compel your listeners to contribute financially to your podcast, it requires a detailed understanding of monetization strategies and their competent implementation, supported by ongoing audience engagement. It's a multifaceted process that combines creativity, business acumen, and a solid grasp of social media mechanics. Below, we delve into an array of practical tips for monetization strategies and their successful execution.

11.1. Understanding Monetization Options

The first step toward generating income from your podcast is to understand the various monetization strategies that are available. Primarily, podcast monetization includes direct and indirect income channels, and often, a blend of these works best.

Direct income channels are those where you receive money directly linked to your podcast. These include sponsorships, advertising (cost per mille, or CPM deals, and cost per acquisition, or CPA deals), premium content, crowdfunding, and listener donations. Sponsorships can be categorized into preroll, midroll, and postroll depending on when the sponsor's message is aired during the podcast. Premium content monetizes the podcast by offering additional value-added content for a price. Crowdfunding refers to receiving funds from a community of listeners or fans who want to contribute towards your podcast's costs.

Indirect channels may not be directly related to the podcast but offer added sources of income. Speaking engagements, selling merchandise, affiliate marketing, hosting events, and coaching or consulting work in your area of expertise fall under this category.

11.2. Implementing Monetization Strategies

Once you're familiar with all the monetization options, the trick lies in selecting which methods align best with your content and audience. Not every method works for every podcast, and understanding your listener base is crucial here. Using survey tools or social media polling can provide insights into what your audience might be receptive to, thereby informing your monetization strategy.

Broadly, the following steps illustrate how to implement monetization strategies for your podcast:

1. Sponsorships: Start by creating a media kit that shares detailed information about your podcast, listener demographics, download stats, and why a company should sponsor you. Once your kit is ready, reach out to potential advertisers that align with your niche.

2. Advertisements: Depending upon your listenership size, you may use podcast advertising platforms or manually manage ads for more profitability. Ensure your advertisements are weaved seamlessly into your podcast to avoid listener drop-off.

3. Premium Content: If offering premium content, ensure it provides genuine value. Whether it's private episodes, extended interviews, or ad-free experiences, your premium content needs to warrant the requested price.

4. Crowdfunding: If you're considering crowdfunding, set up a

platform for listeners to make contributions—Patreon, Kickstarter, and GoFundMe are some popular platforms for this. Just ensure you offer valued incentives for contributors.

5. Indirect Income: For indirect income streams like merchandise or speaking engagements, leverage your social media presence to promote sales and appearances. Social media platforms can be beneficial for highlighting your product offerings or industry expertise.

11.3. Continually Engaging Your Audience

Of course, the only way to sustain and grow your podcast monetization is to continuously engage your audience. This involves regular communication, appreciation for their support, and continual focus on creating quality content that would attract new listeners while retaining the old ones.

Consider the following for maintaining robust audience engagement:

Listener Appreciation: Shoutouts, contests, and giveaways are all great ways of expressing gratitude towards your listeners. The more valued listeners feel, the deeper their connection to your podcast, and thus, the greater their likelihood of supporting it financially.

Monetizing your podcast is a journey that requires time, effort, and a clear understanding of your audience. Use your social media tools wisely, provide valuable content, choose the right monetization strategies, and keep engaging with your community of listeners. This chapter is your primer for navigating this exciting space - absorb, implement, and watch your podcast revenue climb!